TRUTH AND FICTION: NOTES ON (EXCEPTIONAL) FAITH IN ART

Truth and Fiction

Notes on (Exceptional) Faith in Art

Milcho Manchevski

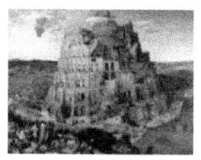

dead letter office

BABEL Working Group

punctum books ✳ brooklyn, ny

TRUTH AND FICTION: NOTES ON (EXCEPTIONAL)
FAITH IN ART
© Milcho Manchevski, 2012.

First published in 2012 by
Dead Letter Office, BABEL Working Group
an imprint of punctum books
Brooklyn, New York
punctumbooks.com

The BABEL Working Group is a collective and
desiring-assemblage of scholar-gypsies with no leaders
or followers, no top and no bottom, and only a middle.
BABEL roams and stalks the ruins of the post-
historical university as a multiplicity, a pack, looking
for other roaming packs and multiplicities with which
to cohabit and build temporary shelters for intellectual
vagabonds.

ISBN-13: 978-0615647104
ISBN-10: 0615647103

Cover Images: from *Street*, a book of still photographs
by Milcho Manchevski, ©1999

. . . all those sweet lies that tell a deeper truth . . .

Table of Contents

*all images from Milcho Manchevski's films
Before the Rain (1994) and *Mothers* (2010),
and from his book of still photographs
Street (1999), unless otherwise noted

Truth and Fiction: Notes On (Exceptional) Faith in Art

Milcho Manchevski

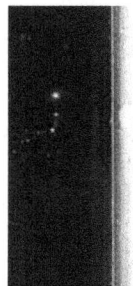 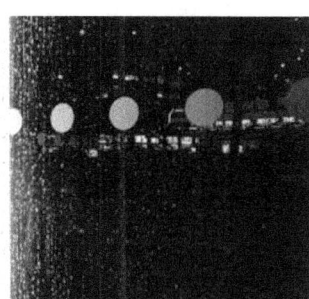

Three years ago I read a fascinating article in the *New York Times*.[1] The article told of Vlado Taneski, a Macedonian journalist. He was a correspondent for two major Macedonian newspapers from a small town, Kičevo. Taneski had been covering the case of several missing

---

[1] See Dan Bilefsky, "Murder Mystery in Macedonia," *The New York Times*, June 23, 2008: http://www.nytimes.com/2008/06/23/world/europe/23iht-macedonia.4.13924930.html.

women in the town. They were all elderly, some of them used to work as cleaning women, and they all lived in the same neighborhood. They could almost see each other's houses from their windows. Taneski wrote that the retired women had all gone missing over a period of three years. Their bodies were later found in plastic bags, discarded in illegal dumps, after having been raped and strangled.

No sooner did Taneski finish writing his most recent report on the unknown serial killer than he was arrested and charged with rape and murder. His DNA was found inside the victims, his wife's hair was found on the clothes the victims' bodies were wrapped in, and the evidence started accumulating.

Taneski was a neighbor. He lived in the same neighborhood as the victims; one of them lived only three houses down from Taneski. All the victims knew him as a friendly neighbor. Their children went to the same schools. They shopped in the same stores. They chatted when they met in the street. Sometimes they would help each other. He may have asked one of them to help him clean his house — his wife lived in the capital, and he was a man alone. He was well-respected as a solid citizen, a journalist, a pillar of his community.

I read the article and pictured Kičevo. It is a small town where people know each other and most live quiet and conservative lives. Many businesses, most of them industrial plants, have closed their doors over the last twenty years. Unemployment is high. Macedonian and Albanian peasants from the countryside come to town on the market days to sell fruit, vegetables and their wares. Children play basketball right next to a car wreck left to rot in the school yard. Attractive women socialize in the downtown cafes.

It was hard to believe that these hideous crimes took place there. We are used to serial killers in America, not in the sleepy Macedonian countryside. And this was not just any serial killer, but a rapist who preyed on retired cleaning women. This is not something one associates with the country I know.

To make things stranger, Taneski not only wrote the articles about the serial killer (including one titled "The Investigation Stalled," where he chides the police for shoddy investigative work), but he also went to see the families of the victims after the women had disappeared and before the bodies were discovered. He went to the families asking for statements, information, and for photographs of the missing women to accompany his articles. The families kindly obliged.

The Vlado Taneski story went around the world: a crime reporter who allegedly killed by night, and wrote about it by day.

Three days later an even more bizarre twist of events was reported. Vlado Taneski was found dead in his prison cell, his head in a bucket of water.[2]

"Now, this is impossible," many readers exclaimed.

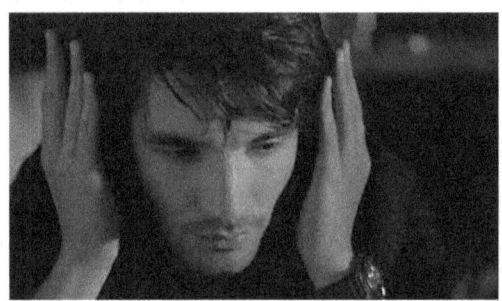

It does seem impossible. Even after two years, the official investigation has not uncovered what had happened that night. The coroner reported that the death was caused by drowning; he reported no signs of violence on Taneski's body or traces of any mind-altering substances in his blood. The press from as far away as Korea, Argentina, and the United States had a field day with the story: a crime

---

[2] See Dan Bilefsky, "Macedonian Murder Suspect Found Dead in Cell," *The New York Times*, June 24, 2008: http: //www.nytimes.com/2008/06/24/world /europe/24macedonia.html, and Helena Smith, "The Shocking Story of the Newspaper Crime Reporter Who Knew Too Much," *The Guardian*, June 23, 2008: http://www.guardian.co.uk/media/2008/jun/24/pre ssandpublishing.international crime.

reporter — suspected of the serial rapes and murders of retired cleaning women whom he was reporting on — ends up dead in a bucket of water in his prison cell.

"Now, this is impossible," is the way many would describe this string of events. "It can't be true," others would say.

I myself read this story in two articles in the *New York Times* in the summer of 2008. I am a storyteller and filmmaker, and I often look at things in real life, or read books and stories, thinking what they would look like if one tried to convert them into films. This story stood out. It was one of those stories that are unbelievable, yet true.

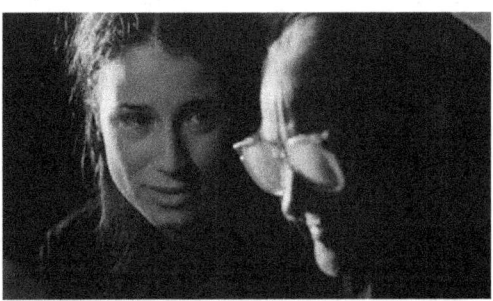

"But, it really happened" — this is something a student of mine once told me after I remarked that his idea for a film did not hold water dramaturgically. His reaction is typical of a common belief which holds that if a film is based on events that really took place the film itself should be believable and believed.

Yet, we have all seen bad and unbelievable films based on real events. And we have all seen great films that were entirely the product of someone's imagination. Films that were so convincing we walked out of the theater crying.

Still, just like my former student, most of us do look at films differently or accept stories in a different way if we believe that they are true. We watch a documentary film in a different way from the way we watch a drama. We read a magazine article in a different way from the way in which we read a short story. Sometimes, we even treat a film that employs actors differently than a regular drama if we are told that the film is based on something that really happened. We treat these works based on truth or reporting on the truth in different ways.

Why?

What is it in our relation to reality or in our relation to what we perceive to be reality that makes us value a work of artifice (an art piece) differently depending on our knowledge or conviction of whether that work of artifice is based on events that really took place?

Mind you — this is not a case of actually observing reality. We are not watching events as they unfold. We are not observing *the truth happen*. What we are observing in a film based on a true story is a highly artificial construct. We are observing actors delivering lines written by a scriptwriter; actors and landscapes and objects filmed in a way determined by the director and by the director of photography and by the production designer. What is left out of the film is determined by the director and the editor.

What we are observing is a work of art — or sometimes just a movie, a piece of light entertainment — with its own inner logic, rhythm, development, and feel. These are all created by the filmmakers, usually deliberately and in line with numerous conventions established between the filmmaker and the viewer, and following the concept or idea the filmmakers had in mind all along.

The same applies to a documentary.

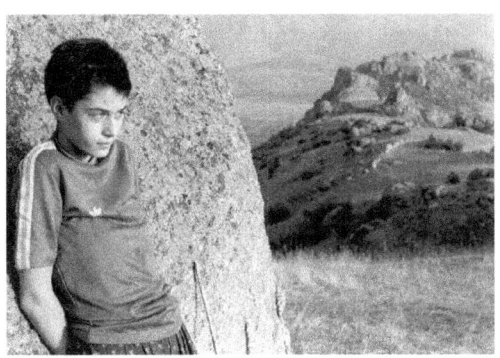

When we watch a documentary we are not observing reality happen in front of our eyes. What we are observing is a film. A documentary film. With its own set of rules and conventions, with its own conclusions as to what exactly happened ("what happened," even in historical accounts, is often up for grabs). These conclusions will sometimes depend on the point of view or on the context the particular film establishes. It will depend on the conclusion the filmmakers have come to while making the film, or — quite often — before even setting out to make the (documentary) film. Regardless of how faithful the filmmakers want to be to the events they are talking about (and which most of them have not witnessed first hand), such a film is a reconstruction. Or a construction.

In addition, the *feel* of the documentary will depend almost entirely on the filmmakers.

The feel is what lies between the lines, what hides behind the story; yet, the feel is precisely what makes us buy the story or discard it; the feel is what makes us like a film or not.

The film will tell its story from a particular point of view, sometimes an "objective" point of view. Yet, reality is never "objective"; it is simply reality. Furthermore, the tone of the film will be determined by the filmmakers: they will choose how the story unfolds (the order might be chronological, or may follow a particular character, or perhaps it saves the surprises for convenient moments in the film, thus creating turning points), the way in which the story is presented (what moment does the film linger on, who are we asked to root for?), the voice-over narration (if there is narration, is it "the voice of God," is it outraged, or ironic, or funny?), the music (if there is music at all), etc. The filmmakers will of course determine the order and length of every single shot, the color grading, the background sounds. All of these elements will shape the film in a way desired by the filmmakers.

All of this (and much more) should make the film an expression or a reflection of the filmmakers. It will also help make the film a richer experience for the regular viewer. More importantly, it would also shape what and how the viewer sees as the story and the "message" of the film.

Yet, it will remove the film one more step from reality — and sometimes even from the truth. Quite often the feeling we would have when we walk out of a film, even if it is documentary, will be very different from the feeling we would have if we were to observe reality instead of watching a film about reality.

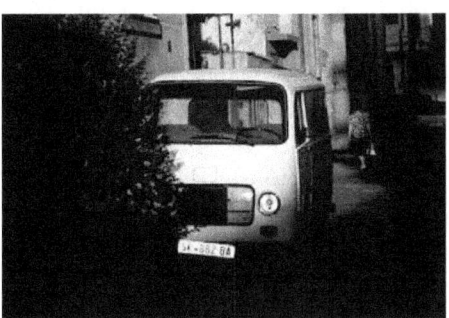

In other words, the film — any film — will be different from the *reality of the truth* it is talking about.

Why then insist on the "faithfulness" or "truthfulness" of the film? No one has ever said, except on advice of their lawyer, "This film was entirely made up. Nothing in it is true." On the contrary, filmmakers often highlight their film's connection to real events or real people, sometimes at the very beginning of the film.

Does it make a film more truthful if it is based on a true story?

Or do we insist on the "faithfulness," the "truthfulness," the "based on a true story" as a way of giving the film more credibility? In the sense of, "This is not just something I dreamed up. It really happened, I am reporting it, and that — handling the truth — makes me a serious member of society." Is that why a lot of serious people prefer documentaries?

As the former student of mine would put it: "But, it really happened!"

Do we use it because the tagline "based on a true story" helps the viewer suspend their disbelief? A viewer walks into a theater and she is supposed to enter the filmmaker's world. It may be a world she likes or a world she doesn't like; it may be a world she believes, or a world she doesn't believe (a world of constructed connections and artificial feelings, instead of a world of coherent vision and compact drama).

The filmmaker needs to gain the viewer's trust. And this is where the filmmaker may reach out for some help and declare: "What I am saying makes sense because it really happened. Trust me."

As every artist knows — or, at least, feels in his or her bones — it is essential to gain the viewer's trust if you expect the work to resonate with the recipient. It is not easy to establish the *field of reality* in a dramatic piece, so using the true story crutch may be helpful in gaining the viewer's trust.

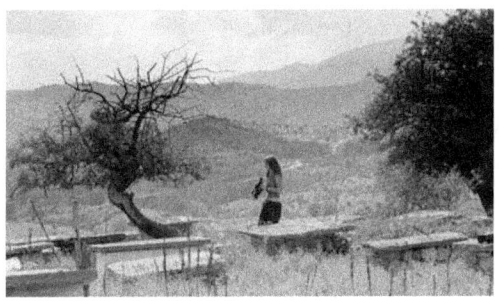

Of course, every work of art has to *earn* the viewer's trust.

The viewer comes to the piece with a level of trust, but the artist has to satisfy — or, if possible, expand upon — this trust. The viewer trusts that the film will be worthy of her expectations, that it will be an emotional, intellectual, and perhaps even a learning experience for her. She trusts that you will take her by the hand and rule her inner world for two hours. She has faith in your ability to deliver, but she also has expectations — she expects something to happen that will move her emotions and also provoke and challenge her intellect.

Now what is interesting about this trust, or faith, is that it goes both ways.

Or, rather, it is something that happens twice: once when the artist creates the piece, and again when the viewer takes it in.

So, the trust is essential for a work of art to:

(1) be created, and,
(2) be consumed.

We are talking here about a high level of trust.

It involves strangers, people who have never met, yet people who feel they can communicate honestly on a profound level. This communication on the part of the artist involves putting his or her inner world on the line, working with one's heart on one's sleeve. It deals with most intimate aspects of one's personality, as art does come from the deepest place in a person.

This trust on the part of the artist does not necessarily involve the viewer at the other end. The artist's real dialogue is perhaps more profound when they communicate with the piece of art they are creating than with the potential inhaler of this art down the line. Which does not make the requirement of deep trust less intense. On the contrary — it is probably easier to lie to the audience than to the work of art itself.

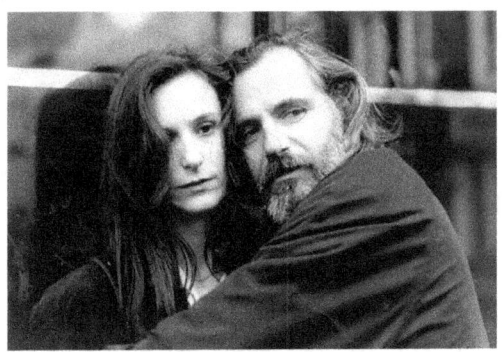

I need to trust that the film I am making is worthwhile in order for me to invest my emotional and, often, physical well-being, plus a minimum of two (and in one case, for myself, seven) years of my life.

Making this choice ("Is it worthwhile or not?") is a process that could involve practical issues (is the film financed, are there any "names" attached, who is distributing the film, is it based on a successful book, is this a popular genre, etc.?). For me, though, it is more important whether a film I am about to embark on making speaks to me. Does it excite me months or even years after I originally had the idea to make the film? This is not really something you can squeeze into a rational explanation — the simplest way to describe it is to compare it to falling in love. Both making art and falling in love are about translating impulses and feelings into actions in the material world.

Most importantly, I have to have faith in this undertaking in order for myself to strip down to the core and bare my soul, my real emotions, and my deepest thoughts on essential issues, such as "why love?" or "why live?" to name just two.

It is important that I strip down in order to reach the emotional and conceptual essence of what I want to say, even when my work does not necessarily seem personal. Yet, it is this personal involvement that provides the basis for art. Again, I don't need to talk directly about my personal concerns, but I need to invest myself into my art for it to gain that breath of life. Craft alone is not enough.

Of course, every piece of art has to contain the truth. But, not the truth of "what happened." It needs to contain the truth of how things are — and the difference between "what happened" and "how things are" is what is important. Is it the events (and by extension, the facts) of what happened, or is it the emotional and conceptual underpinning and thus understanding of how things are?

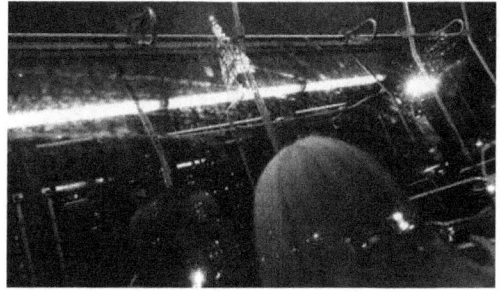

While making my art, I am communicating with my piece, not with the audience or with myself. My commitment is to the piece of art alone. Nothing can make my faith in my work relative. The artwork and my relationship to it are not negotiable.

It is a little bit like a musician on stage, playing his instrument with the light in his eyes. He is wrapped up in the music, oblivious and vulnerable to whatever lies beyond it, and he becomes aware of the audience only when they start applauding.

The honesty of my relationship with my piece, plus my ability to communicate this onto the work of art, is what inspires faith in the viewer.

For her part, the viewer — as I've said — comes to the battlefield, or to the bedroom, or to the cinema theater with herself also exposed, even if to a smaller degree. She comes and says, "I like this kind of film, I am investing my time, two hours of my life, and my emotional expectations in your work. I believe you to the point of crying because an actor on the screen pretends to be dying. Do this for me."

Both of us are taking a major leap of faith.

What the filmmaker does with this faith is essential. If the artist takes it seriously and repays it multiple times with his or her work, it becomes a type of *love*.

I approach the film I am creating with faith. The viewer approaches the film she is watching with faith. There is no film and no art without this faith.

This is it: faith in the art piece itself to transcend the moment of creating and the moment of inhaling art.

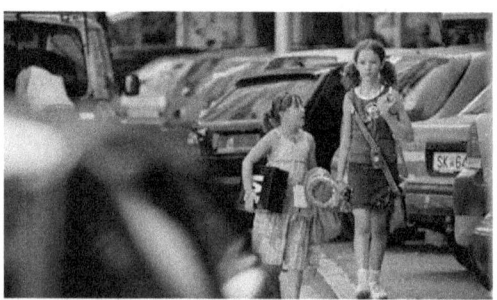

A perverse question floats up to the surface here:

Did Vlado Taneski (if he was, indeed, the real murderer) need the reality of the rapes and murders so that he could write about them? It is as if he could not just *write* about them, or invent them, but he needed to report about them. Could that be part of what happened?

Not too long ago a viewer asked me why I decided to make the film about Vlado Taneski as a documentary?

Yes, I did make a film, *Mothers*, about the case of the Kičevo reporter who died in a bucket of water in prison, after being charged with raping and killing the retired cleaning women he was writing about.

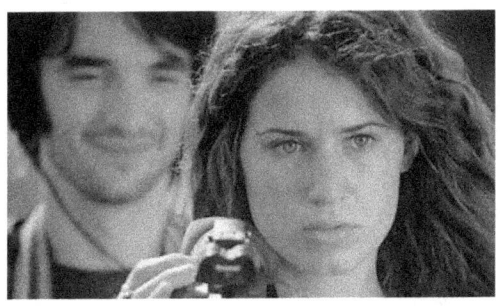

However, the story of Vlado Taneski, presented as a documentary, was only part of the film, only one of three completely unrelated stories that comprise my film *Mothers*. The other two segments are dramatic fictions, with actors and scripted dialogue. Yet, they are both based on real events. What unfolds in these two fiction segments of the film is based on what happened to two friends of mine. Thus all three stories were based on real events, but they were treated differently; I applied radically different cinematic approaches.

Truth is extremely important, and I fulfilled my obligation to it in *Mothers* by trying to get to the bottom of what happened in these complicated series of events that came from my friends' lives and also the newspapers, both in terms of facts and context. I also tried to give everybody involved a chance to share their experiences and perspectives. Yet, this attempt to tell the facts and to satisfy different perspectives was not the most important thing.

What was more important was the following: I was trying to ask questions about the nature of truth, rather than trying to get at or reveal the so-called "truth, the whole truth, and nothing but the truth." We see different permutations of truth and lies in the three parts of *Mothers*.

In a structuralist manner, we are finally faced with considering the medium itself, the font the poem is printed in, the texture of the canvas, the clash and marriage of the documentary and fictional approaches in one and the same piece.

So, *Mothers* is comprised of three unrelated stories — two of which are dramatic fictions and one a documentary.

In the first story, two nine-year-old girls report a flasher to the police even though they never saw him. In the second story, three filmmakers meet the only residents of a deserted village — an elderly brother and sister who have not spoken to each other in 16 years. And in the third story, retired cleaning women are found raped and strangled in a small town. In a way, you could say that the fiction slowly turns into a documentary.

The film is intended to work like the triptychs you see in churches or museums, where the three paintings function as one unit and work and riff in relation to each other. The three paintings are complete on their own, but they really tell a story only when seen as a whole. When you put them side by side, their differences are emphasized, as are their similarities. We are asked to consider them in a new light.

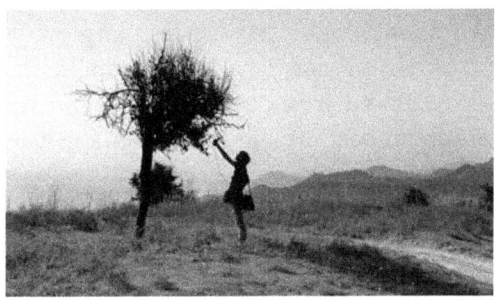

The most obvious link between the three stories in *Mothers* is the fact that all three narratives portray dark aspects of life in contemporary Macedonia. Yet, these stories could easily take place almost anywhere in the world. What also links them is the interest in victims and perpetrators, and in lies and truth.

However, the more interesting link between the three is how they are connected by tone and theme. I am not interested in narrative devices where one story neatly dovetails into another. Been there, done that. With *Mothers*, I was more interested in a Spartan, austere film, where the connections would be made in the mind of the beholder, and these connections would not necessarily be narrative. In the end, what matters most is the complex *feeling* created in the mind of the viewer who is looking at all three, seemingly unrelated stories, together.

The stories are about the nature of truth rather than about truth itself. The more we learn about the truth, the less important the factual truth becomes, and the more important the emotional truth of a living person is. The facts are important, but in the end, the love and the suffering and what to do with them is more important than the facts.

These three stories in *Mothers* never really come together on the narrative level. The fact that they remain unconnected plot-wise, and, more importantly, the fact that I mix drama and documentary (or as some people would have it, "truth and fiction") is not very common. Documentary and drama usually don't mix. When they do, the drama is often just a re-enactment of what happens in the documentary, as if the documentary needs clarifications or as if it needs more convincing (or "entertaining") ways of making its so-called "points."

I wanted to combine these two approaches, two genres, two kinds of filmmaking. I felt there was no need to be restricted in the way I used the material, in the style and approach, the way we have been taught. Painting has been using found objects for a long time now. Many great artists have been incorporating found objects in their art pieces. The shock of seeing an unexpected other medium (found object) within a painting or sculpture adds a new level to the experience. Artists like Picasso and Rauschenberg have created beautiful works of art by using objects seemingly incongruous with a work of painterly art, such as a blanket, linoleum, bicycle handlebars, stuffed goat or newspaper photographs. Yet, what really matters in the final piece is not the shock that we are looking at unexpected material where we don't expect it, but rather the fact that the found object has been incorporated into the art piece in a way that feels seamless in terms of the overall idea and result and contributes to a great piece of art.

In other words, the novelty of incorporating found objects in a work of art (or of mixing drama and documentary in a substantial way) is not enough. The art itself still needs to work. It needs to be good.

Why couldn't film expand the technological and artistic means at its disposal by freely mixing documentary and fiction? Why do those two approaches (documentary and fiction) have to be considered mutually exclusive? Is it something in the nature of our perception of the work of art, the work of telling stories, of creating something out of nothing that makes us treat the drama and documentary as separate animals? After all, a story is just a story, isn't it?

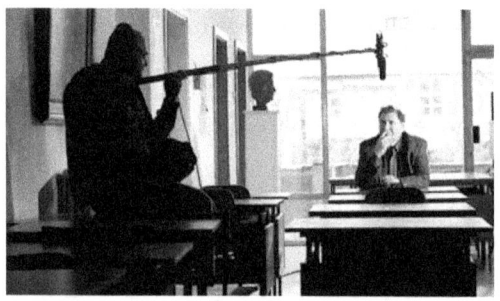

This is where we neatly circle back to an earlier point: We watch a documentary film in a different way from the way we watch a drama. We read a magazine article in a different way from the way in which we read a short story. Sometimes, we even treat a film that employs actors differently than a regular drama when we are told that the film is based on something that really happened. We treat these works based on truth or reporting on the truth in a different way.

Why?

I am not sure.

الله

Several years ago I screened my first film, *Before the Rain* (1994), at Brown University in Providence, Rhode Island. That film consists of three love stories set in London and Macedonia against the backdrop of tension and potential violence that is about to erupt, both in London and in Macedonia. Some of the tension is caused, "excused," or enhanced by ethnic intolerance. However, there was no violence in Macedonia at the time. The film was made eight years before an ethnic conflict — or what was being explained as an ethnic conflict — actually erupted in Macedonia.

Yet, since *Before the Rain* came from Macedonia, and Macedonia had only recently declared its independence from Yugoslavia, which itself was at that time torn apart by wars of civil disintegration along ethnic lines, many people looked for clues about the nature of the actual wars in this film.

I did not feel that watching *Before the Rain* would help anyone understand the facts of these actual wars in Yugoslavia. (For starters, there were no politicians in *Before the Rain*.) My intention was to talk about other human issues that concerned me, not to explain a particular war. I wanted to talk and ask questions about how to be honest, about self-sacrifice, about forbidden love, about empathy, about the relationship between the individual and the group, about how to behave when one is caught in the jaws of history.

I conceived and perceived *Before the Rain* as a piece of fiction applicable to any place in the world. And, indeed, viewers from very different places did come up to me to tell me that the film had made them think of their respective homelands, that it could easily have taken place in their homelands.

With this in mind, I told the viewers before the screening at Brown University that the film they were about to see was not a documentary about Macedonia; nor was it a documentary about the wars in what used to be Yugoslavia. It is not a documentary at all, I told the audience. Satisfied that I helped frame the film for the viewers, I settled down.

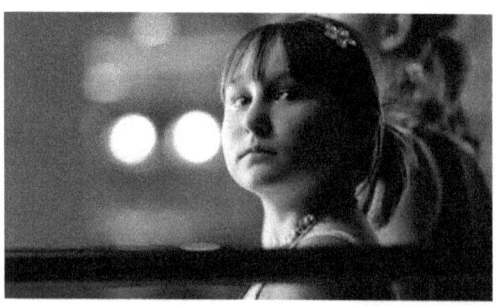

After the screening I came forward for a Q&A session. An elderly woman raised her hand and asked the first question: "Did what we see in the film actually happen to you or to anyone in your family?"

Relying on whether something "really happened" or valorizing documentaries over drama only because they are documentaries, or praising a film because of the subject matter it treats and not because of its essence, soul, mind and muscle feels like a cheat. A crutch.

It seems that some of us need to know that something is "true" only because it would help our faith — our faith in the power of the piece of art. Yet, whether something is "true" or not is an external category. Sure, it can ease our way into trusting the plane of reality of the particular work, but it cannot substitute for the lack of heart and soul.

Did the woman in Providence like *Before the Rain* more because she thought it was "true"?

I don't think so. As I stated above, we've all seen many "based on a true story" films that were no good. We didn't like them. I would like to believe that the woman in Providence liked the film because of the film itself.

I believe that deep down our experience with a film does not really depend on whether the film speaks of events that truly happened or not. Yes, both viewers and filmmakers often put a lot of stock in whether something is based on a real story. Still, I am convinced that the emotional charge we get out of a great work of art is mainly related to that particular work of art, to that particular piece of artifice, to that particular object, that particular sound or that particular image or that particular concept which we call a piece of art.

Faith that needs some sort of outside support ("based on a true story") seems suspect to me. Seems like *faith lite*.

I think that when we like a work of art, we like it because of what it does to our body and soul while we are receiving it. We like it because it wakes us up, because it lifts us up and takes us with it, because it says, "this is what things feel like, this is what being on the face of this Earth is like, this is what things are like or can be like." In other words, because of what we are experiencing on a profound level while watching, reading or listening; we like it because we trust the *plane of reality created by the work itself*, we trust its inner logic and integrity, we have faith in what happens while we give ourselves to this piece of art.

In other words, it is beside the point whether a work of art is real or fiction. It is the viewer's faith in the particular piece of art that it has earned which makes it work.

We accept the artistic truth because we have faith in it.

In order to accept art, we need exceptional faith.

The rest is up to the art itself.

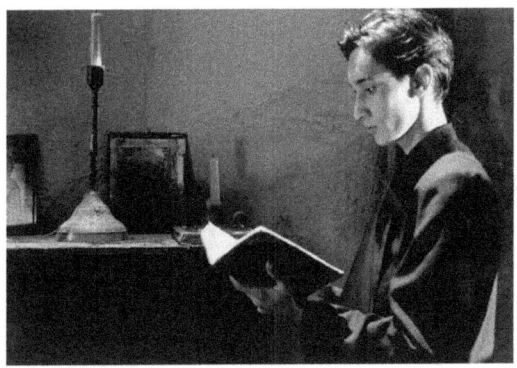

Afterword: Truth Approaches, Reality Affects

Adrian Martin

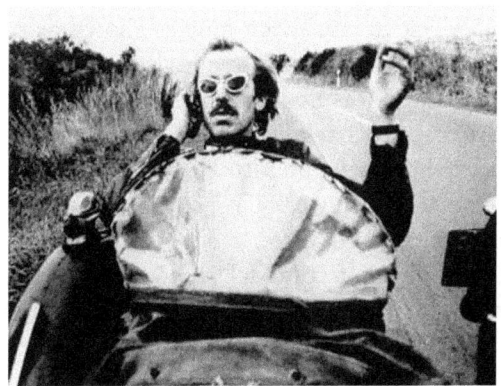

Figure 1. still image from Wim Wenders, *Kings of the Road* (1976)

Like Milcho Manchevski — but more from the angle of being a critic or a teacher, rather than a highly accomplished filmmaker — I have frequently been stunned, bemused, or frankly puzzled at what people take or experience to be *real* in any given film. This is not, in any simple or primary way, a matter of the conventional distinction in cinema between documentary and fiction; nor is it confined to any particular filmic genre. The *moment of truth* — to use the title of Francesco Rosi's 1965 documentary on bullfighting, made (as its DVD distributor Criterion proudly boasts) by a "great Italian truth seeker" — can impress itself upon viewers in the least likely contexts.

I tried to test this business once, on and with my students at university. I devised a course that was called, somewhat cryptically and open-endedly, "Truth, Fiction, Belief." From week to week, the movies shown as part of the curriculum were a surprise, an improvisation: there was no guiding thread beyond the multiple paradoxes generated by these three terms when brought into collision. Is truth in cinema just what we believe or feel to be true — something, therefore, not objective but subjective? Can fiction deliver forth a truth and, if so, what kind? Where do the various modes and schools of documentary — not to mention all the various realist or neo-realist movements in fictional film — sit on the continuum between ideal transparency and total fabrication? And what's naturalism? Manchevski sifts through a number of these issues, from his point of view, in the provocative essay you have just read.

For my part, I discovered that the class on truth, fiction, and belief kept turning up the most bizarre responses in participants. On the one hand, the American *cinéma-vérité*, or 'direct cinema,' exemplars of the early 1960s — about elections, electrocutions, or pop stars on tour — impressed my students as real (even hyperreal), but only when the screen dissolved in a frenzy of bodies shoving and screaming, uncontainable within the camera lens. On the other hand, they came away from a screening of Wim Wenders's almost three-hour long *Kings of the Road* (1976) with a single, indelible memory: when, in the midst of a banal, plotless stretch, one of the uncommunicative male heroes dropped his jeans, crouched down in the sand, and took a shit right before the camera, *that* was definitely real! No cutaways or special effects there; we all saw it with our own eyes! (Ah, the innocence of those analog days . . . .)

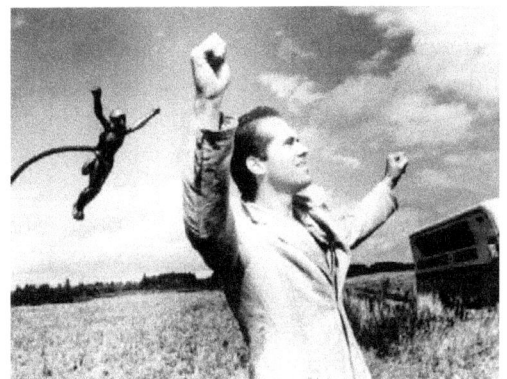

Figure 2. still image from Wim Wenders, *Kings of the Road* (1976)

Some students were disconcerted when I voiced my analytic conclusion: the real, for them, obviously happens in only two screen registers, at two stark extremes: either total catastrophe, or absolute mundanity. Everything else in the middle was mere fiction.

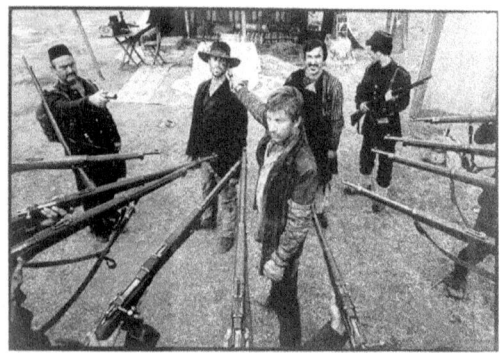

Figure 3. still image from Milcho Manchevski, *Dust* (2001)

Manchevski, like the experimentalist James Benning, likes to point at the rectangular movie screen and assert, in any public situation, that it's all, in some sense, a fiction, all constructed: at every point and every level, there is art and craft, contrivance and manipulation. There should be, in an ideal world, no shame in that; it's just a fact, it's what happens when you assemble anything with a mind to its structure, its point, and its impact. This is certainly what Manchevski elaborates when he reminds us of the powers of framing, of montage, of sound design, of even the least seemingly rehearsed or staged effusion of human behaviour that, be-fore a camera, can become, almost magically,

telling or emblematic. As the teacher-
filmmaker-essayist Jean-Pierre Gorin once
formulated it (in his specific case, in relation to
the fiction films of Maurice Pialat, but it works
for all cinema), every director does three basic
things with his or her material.[1]

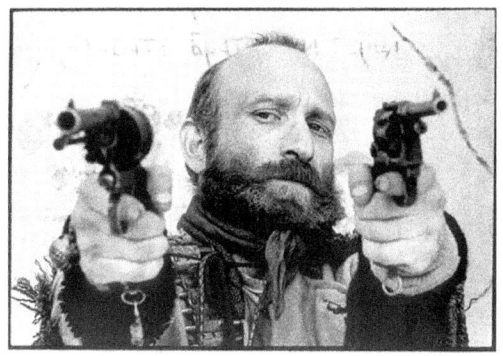

Figure 4. still image from Milcho Manchevski, *Dust*
(2001)

In the first place, there is the effort to *catalyse*
or create some kind of interesting or meaning-
ful situation in the real space in front of the
camera, a process that may have started long
before filming begins. In the second place, and
still as the camera rolls, there is some manner
of *maneuvering*: a particular, decisive choice of
angle or style of shooting, some distance or
perspective chosen in relation to what is
occurring. In the third place, as the film goes

[1] Jean-Pierre Gorin, *"L'Enfance-nue," Film Comment*
40.3 (May-June 2004): 36.

into postproduction (editing, sound design, etc.), there is the necessary *working* of and on the material gathered: finding or inventing a form for it, creating the global, aesthetic context in which it will be received by audiences.

What Manchevski and Gorin are saying, each in their own ways, makes me think that what is crucially missing from a lot of discussion of documentary (no matter how "dramatically reconstructed" or essayistic it may be) is a simple but flexible application of the famous Lacanian triad of Real, Symbolic, and Imaginary. You capture something on camera and place it in your film. Is it automatically the Real? No, because the Real is going to be something essentially fleeting, elusive, hard to grasp and even harder to take in. But, Real or not (and whether you, as a filmmaker, like it or not), the footage is going to inevitably come freighted with two other layers: Symbolic and Imaginary. It's going to reflect, and be embedded in, a whole range of social codings you can only fitfully control — that's the Symbolic realm. And it's going to be completely shaped, even warped, by the dreams and drives, the projections and phantasmic scenarios that impel you to pick up a camera and keep it trained on someone or something in the first place. That's your Imaginary at work, but bear in mind what Serge Daney once said: "Fantasies are the least personal thing in the world. They are collective. A dream is only a montage of coded elements, obeying precise, impersonal rules."[2]

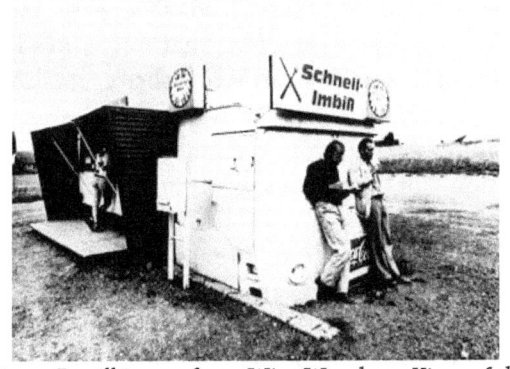

Figure 5. still image from Wim Wenders, *Kings of the Road* (1976)

As someone involved with theory and critique, I came to a position not unlike Manchevski's via the powerful arguments, which initially circulated throughout the 1960s and 1970s, concerning *reality-effects* (Roland Barthes) and *truth-effects* (Michel Foucault). There's no such absolute, universal thing as Reality or Truth; there are only instances, effects, performances (in the widest sense) that strike us as such. A whole machinery of social persuasion, of contextual discourse, is needed to deliver us to

---

[2] Serge Daney and Philippe Garrel, "Dialogue," *Cahiers du cinema* 443/444 (May 1991): 60 (my translation).

these precisely coded moments, which are (as it turns out) pitifully time-bound: the reality-effects of yesterday are, in most cases, the comedic clichés of today, easily seen for the constructions they are. Today, we are more likely to grasp these *effects* that once fooled us as also *affects*: the heart's complicity, stealthily engineered, is never far way from the clever techniques that, for a moment, conjured an illusion of immediacy, transparency, and authenticity.

There is a wonderful phrase in English: *truth approaches*. It can mean a few different things, depending on whether you take *approach* (just like *affect*) as noun or verb. It could be referring to diverse approaches to truth itself, or to something happening: look out, the plot thickens, the truth is approaching. Either way, the phrase underlines something dramatic, theatrical and performative about Truth when it is in the process of hitting us: there is always going to be something rhetorical about those moments when the truth is finally revealed, and just as dramatically withdraws itself. In fact, I recall a clever, Warholian video art piece made almost three decades ago in Melbourne by Ralph Traviato, based exactly on this theme. It was titled *The Truth Approaches* (1983): in it, a series of performers, filmed in simple, static mid-shots, went through the motions of certain, banal actions (checking their watch, straightening their tie, stirring a cup of tea, etc.). Every time, a certain cumulative effect of waiting, of suspense, was produced in those who watched the video: what's up, what's about to slip out from hiding here? Of course, the video was, ultimately, nothing but the demonstration of this seductive rhetoric in the artful process of enacting itself. And every kind of time-based media is going about its business of producing such an audiovisual rhetoric, each moment of the day.

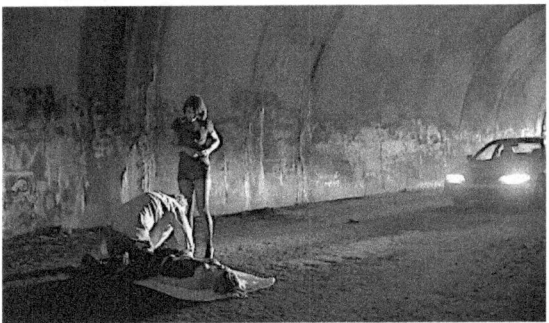

Figure 6. still image from Monte Hellman, *Road to Nowhere* (E1 Films, 2010)

Manchevski alights upon the most puzzling of all the tricks associated with this kind of rhetoric: the crazy phrase, usually solemnly declared in writing at the start of a film or TV programme 'this is a true story,' or 'based on a true story,' or 'these events really happened,' or some such suitably dramatic variation. Jerry Lewis was already sending this one up rotten in 1962, when he began his *The Ladies' Man* with the print-out: "The picture you are about to see is NOT TRUE, only the names have been changed, because the lawyers worry a lot." And, almost forty years on from that, Monte Hellman *ends* his labyrinthine, Robbe-Grillet-style, Chinese-box noir head-scratcher *Road to Nowhere* with the obviously risible boast of "This is a true story," clearly meant to indicate the exact opposite of what it says. But to no avail: as double-whammy truth/reality-effects go, this true-story business has proven staying power.

I was once involved, at script stage, with a big-budget production and I was given a chance to see how this True Story process really works itself out. People begin with what is, indeed, a true story: something that has been in all the newspapers, TV shows, and online. Something immediately known and recognised by a vast audience. Then, for twenty different reasons (from 'dramatic license' to legal complications), the filmmaking team, in the planning phase, begin departing from "just the facts, ma'am." First, the names are changed. Then, certain "characters" are combined. Maybe genders and races are switched. Then the events themselves are tinkered with, usually in order to fit one or other of the preordained "story arcs" beloved of the Hollywood screenwriting manuals. The initial set-up, the complicating factors, even the ultimate outcome, can be tampered with, often arriving at something with precious little resemblance to the so-called true story. (I am sure we can all think of numerous examples.) At several points in this process, I feebly protested to the producers: we have by now ventured so far away from the true-life premise, in every particular, so why don't we just wipe the slate clean and write a fiction that pleases us? Oh no, what heresy! After all, it's a true story! . . . And, above all, it is the market-lure of that declaration, emblazoned on-screen at the start, which is going to secure some sort of effect/ affect that is deemed absolutely necessary to both the dramatic and commercial performance of the piece. (I didn't last long on that project.)

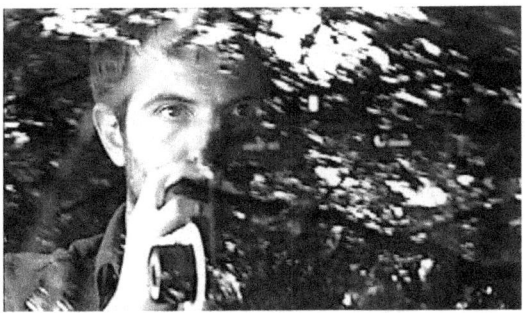

Figure 7. still image from Monte Hellman, *Road to Nowhere* (E1 Films, 2010)

Manchevski wisely separates the commotion around reality-effects from the deeper issue about truth. Reality, realism, the reality-effect, whether comically obvious or deviously surreptitious: ultimately, these are neither here nor there for him. Truth is what matters — but not as a mere, performative effect/affect.

To provisionally resolve the paradoxes that so bedevilled my students and myself once upon a time, Milcho Manchevski adds a necessary and enabling fourth term: Truth, Fiction, Belief . . . and Faith. Indeed, he refers to an *exceptional* faith, not just some run-of-the-mill, obligatory, routinized practice of faith (or worship). Exceptional faith not in an ideology, a cause, or a cultural movement, but in Art itself. And, as we know, faith demands a leap — a leap into what is not yet known or felt, seen, or heard.

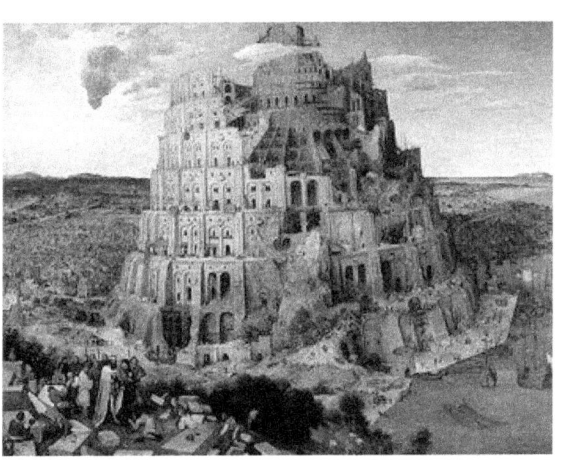

W. dreams, like Phaedrus, of an army of thinker-friends, thinker-lovers. He dreams of a thought-army, a thought-pack, which would storm the philosophical Houses of Parliament. He dreams of Tartars from the philosophical steppes, of thought-barbarians, thought-outsiders. What distances would shine in their eyes!

~Lars Iyer

www.babelworkinggroup.org

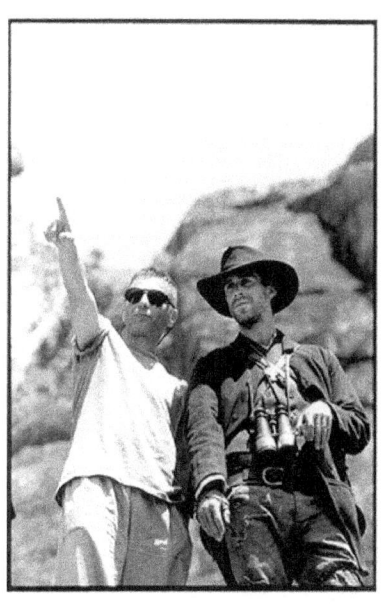

Milcho Manchevski has written and directed the feature films *Before the Rain* (nominated for an Academy Award and winner of over 30 film awards, including the Golden Lion for Best Film), *Dust*, *Shadows*, and *Mothers*, and over 50 short forms, including *Tennessee* for *Arrested Development*. He has also been a director on HBO's *The Wire*. His fiction, essays and op-ed pieces have appeared in *New American Writing*, *La Repubblica*, *Corriere Della Sera*, *Sineast*, *The Guardian*, *Suddeutsche Zeitung*, and *Pravda*, among other publications. He has authored a (very small) book of fiction, *The Ghost of My Mother*, and two books of photographs, *Street* and *Five Drops of Dream*, which accompanied two photo exhibitions. Manchevski has lectured at a number of universities, cinematheques, art museums and art institutes, most notably as a Head of Directing Studies at NYU's Tisch School of the Arts' Graduate Film program.